THE HISTORY OF EXPLORATION
CAPTAIN COOK
& HIS EXPLORATION OF THE PACIFIC

NEW
FOREST
PRESS

Publisher: Tim Cook
Editor: Guy Croton
Designer: Carol Davis
Production Controller: Ed Green
Production Manager: Suzy Kelly

ISBN: 978-1-84898-303-8
Library of Congress Control Number: 2010925457
Tracking number: nfp0003

U.S. publication © 2010 New Forest Press
Published in arrangement with Black Rabbit Books

PO Box 784, Mankato, MN 56002
www.newforestpress.com

Printed in the USA
9 8 7 6 5 4 3 2 1

CONTENTS

Greenland

NORTH
AMERICA

Atlantic
Ocean

N

SOUTH
AMERICA

To England
To England

THE VOYAGES OF CAPTAIN COOK

Russia

EUROPE

China

India

FRICA

Indian
Ocean

To England

Australia

Antarctica

KEY
1st journey 1768–1771
2nd journey 1772–1775
3rd journey 1776–1780

THE WORLD OF COOK

When Cook was born in 1728, Europeans had only a rough knowledge of the Americas, Africa, India, and the Far East. New Zealand and most of the Pacific were unknown, as well as all of Australia except for the west coast. Europeans had long dreamed of finding a Northwest Passage to the East around northern Canada. It was also believed that an inhabitable Great Southern Continent might lie where we now know there is only the frozen waste of Antarctica. Exploration was limited, partially by the hardships, malnutrition, and scurvy of long sailing voyages, and by the simple methods of navigation. Thus, few British seamen had crossed the Pacific Ocean since Sir Francis Drake was the first Englishman to do so in 1577–1580.

TERRESTRIAL GLOBE, AROUND 1740

Made when Cook was around 12 years old, this shows the world before the explorations of the 1760s. Although the shapes of India and Southeast Asia are clearly marked, the east coast of Australia is missing, along with most of New Zealand and Van Diemen's Land, as Tasmania was known.

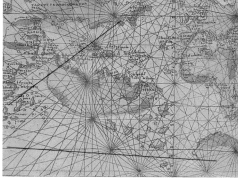

A WORLD MAP BY FRANCESCO ROSSELLI, AROUND 1508

Printed around 15 years after Christopher Columbus returned from discovering the "New World," Rosselli's map suggests the Americas but no Pacific Ocean. A Great Southern Continent was then thought to exist to balance the weight of the northern lands.

LIKE THE *GOLDEN HIND*

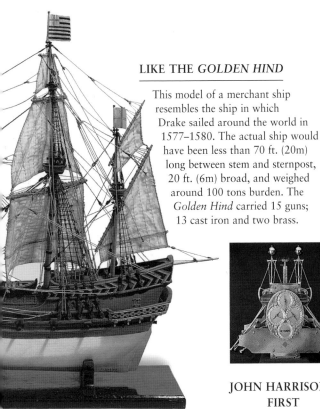

This model of a merchant ship resembles the ship in which Drake sailed around the world in 1577–1580. The actual ship would have been less than 70 ft. (20m) long between stem and sternpost, 20 ft. (6m) broad, and weighed around 100 tons burden. The *Golden Hind* carried 15 guns; 13 cast iron and two brass.

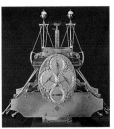

JOHN HARRISON'S FIRST CHRONOMETER

A large prize was offered to anyone who could solve the problem of finding longitude at sea. Harrison, a Yorkshire carpenter and clockmaker, did so by developing an accurate sea-clock to calculate longitude from time. This is his first experimental model, completed in 1735.

MARINER'S ASTROLABE

Seamen used astrolabes between around 1470 and 1700 to determine their latitude by measuring the height above the horizon of the Sun at noon, or the North Star at night. This astrolabe was found in 1845 on the island of Valentia, Ireland, and is presumed to come from the wreck of a ship from the Spanish Armada, in 1588.

CAPTAIN COOK -A TIMELINE-

~1492~

Christopher Columbus discovers central America

~1577~

Sir Francis Drake starts his voyage around the world

~1588~

The Spanish Armada threatens Britain with invasion

~1714~

Board of Longitude established to promote solutions for finding longitude (east/west position) at sea

~1728~

Cook born at Marton-in-Cleveland, north Yorkshire, England

~1729~

John Harrison starts building his first experimental chronometer

SIR FRANCIS DRAKE

When he led a voyage around the world in 1577–1580, Drake was only the second man to have done so. Crossing the Pacific, his ship, the *Golden Hind*, was out of sight of land for 68 days, preventing his men getting the fresh food which kept scurvy at bay. Having sailed with 164 men, he returned with less than 60. Shipwreck and battles with Spanish vessels also contributed to his losses.

SHIPS & SAILING

The crews of the early voyages of exploration faced many dangers. Not only did they have to put up with cramped conditions and only a small supply of food and water (which was often bad), but they were usually sailing into the unknown with little idea where they were and how fast they were traveling. Perhaps it is not surprising, therefore, that many early explorers had to face mutiny—and this was also a problem in Cook's day. Today, ships have little trouble locating their exact position. Accurate maps, clocks, and global positioning satellites (GPS) mean that sailors can tell where they are to within a few feet. Sailors hundreds of years ago were not so fortunate.

MAGNETIC COMPASS

It was vitally important that the sailors crossing the Atlantic Ocean knew exactly in what direction they were sailing. On a clear day or night, either the Sun or the North Star were used. They could also use a magnetic compass. The magnetic field around Earth meant that a magnetized needle floating in water would always point northward.

DEAD RECKONING

If a navigator knew where his ship sailed from, what its speed was, the direction the ship was traveling in, and how long they had been traveling, then it was possible to calculate how far they had traveled by "dead-reckoning" and so find their position. However, winds and tides meant that this was only an approximate way of figuring out the ship's position. The early explorer Christopher Columbus was regarded as a great navigator because of his skill with "dead-reckoning."

MORE ON THE ASTROLABE

Up until Cook's time, every navigator made use of the astrolabe (similar to this Arabic example). It could be used to find out how far north or south of the equator (latitude) the ship was. It worked by measuring the height of the North Star or noon Sun from the ship. Once the height was known, then the navigator could calculate how far north or south he was.

THE CROSSSTAFF

In the early days of exploration, the simplest way to measure the latitude of a ship was to use an instrument called a crossstaff. It had a crossbar for sighting and a rod with measurements cut into the side. The crossbar would be lined up between the Sun or North Star and the horizon. The measurements of the long piece of wood would then tell the navigator the angle of the Sun or star from the horizon. From this, he could figure out his latitude. There is considerable danger in staring at the Sun for too long. In 1595, Captain John Davis invented the backstaff, which used mirrors and shadows so that navigators did not risk being injured.

TELLING THE TIME

For early navigators to calculate a ship's position, it was vital that they knew what time of day it was. Sailors would be given the job of watching a large sand-filled hourglass (similar to the 17th-century example, shown here). It normally emptied after 30 minutes and then a bell would be rung so that everybody on board knew what the time was.

THE QUADRANT

Alongside the astrolabe, early explorers including Cook took quadrants with them. When Ferdinand Magellan started on his famous voyage around the world in 1519, he took seven astrolabes and 21 quadrants. Quadrants basically did the same job as astrolabes. They worked by lining up one arm with the horizon and then moving a movable arm so that it was pointing at either the Sun or North Star. The angle between these two arms could then be used to calculate the ship's latitude. It could only really work when the sea was calm and still.

NAVIGATION

In these days of radar, computer technology, and satellites, it is easy to underestimate the great navigational skills of the early seafaring explorers. For the large part they were sailing uncharted seas and had to estimate their position as best they could, using only the positions of heavenly bodies to guide them. Until the development of more refined instruments, such as the chronometer in the mid-18th century, navigation was a very inexact science and relied heavily on the observational skills of the individual. Needless to say, there were many accidents, particularly if the ships were blown off-course into unknown waters by bad weather.

GUIDED BY THE STARS

During the 16th century the crossstaff became commonly used to calculate a ship's latitude (north-south position) at night. It comprised two pieces of wood, similar in appearance to a crossbow, with graduated scales marked along the length. By observing the angle between the horizon and the North (or Pole) Star and taking a reading off the scale, coupled with a compass reading, the ship's approximate position could be calculated. Shown here is a buckstaff, invented about 1594, for measuring the height of the sun for the same purpose.

THE "MARINER'S MIRROUR"

Following Magellan's, and later Drake's, circumnavigation of the world, it became possible more accurately to assess the Earth's size, which led in turn to the production of more accurate charts. The first sea atlas to be published in England, in 1588, was the *Mariner's Mirrour*. It was a collection of maps and charts showing the known coastlines of the world, derived from Dutch originals. By the 18th century mapmaking and charting techniques had become far more sophisticated, and Cook himself was responsible for creating many important charts.

LODESTONE

One of the main problems facing early navigators was accurately calculating a ship's longitude (east-west position). Here, the astronomer-mathematician Flavius tries to do so by floating a piece of lodestone (a form of iron oxide) in a bowl of water, whilst making calculations. By the mid-18th century, advances were such that Cook was able to calculate longitude with unprecedented accuracy.

STEERING BY THE SUN

This view shows an Elizabethan navigator trying to calculate the ship's latitude by use of a compass and an early form of quadrant to measure the angle of the sun's rays. However, precise timekeeping was necessary to ensure the accuracy of the calculations so at best a ship's position could only be approximated. The first fully successful sea-clock (chronometer) was not developed until 1759.

DRAKE'S DIAL

By Elizabethan times, compasses and other astronomical instruments had become quite sophisticated, as can be seen in this beautifully crafted astronomical compendium. It was made of brass in 1569 by Humphrey Cole, one of the finest scientific instrument makers of the time. The compendium comprised a compass, along with lunar and solar dials which, as well as being an astronomical aid, enabled the user to calculate the time. Engraved on the casing were the latitudes of many important ports around the world. Cook's later instruments were far more advanced, but were based on the same scientific principles.

NAVIGATION
-A TIMELINE-

~1675~

Charles II founds the Royal Observatory, Greenwich.

~1714~

Board of Longitude established to promote solutions for finding longitude at sea.

~1729~

John Harrison begins building his first experimental chronometer.

~1761~

Harrison's fourth chronometer (H4) is successfully trialed.

GETTING YOUR BEARINGS

The ancient Chinese discovered that lodestone is naturally magnetic and if suspended on a string will always point to the north. Early navigators made good use of this natural material but it was somewhat crude. Sometime in the 12th century, European navigators discovered that a needle could be similarly magnetized by stroking it with a lodestone. This discovery eventually led to the development of more sophisticated and accurate compasses, with the needle balanced on a central pivot. The example shown here is encased in an ivory bowl and dates from about 1580.

LIFE ON BOARD

Life on board ship in the 16th to the 18th centuries was extremely harsh and the pay (which was frequently in arrears) was very poor. But, faced with abject poverty on land at a time when many country people were being forcibly ejected from their land because of changing farming practices, many had little option. A fair proportion of a ship's crew would also have been criminals escaping justice, which often led to problems with discipline. The mortality rate amongst an average crew was very high and it would be considered normal for a ship to return to port with only a quarter of the men left alive. To ensure they had enough men left to make the return journey most captains oversubscribed when signing on a new crew, but this in itself led to problems of overcrowding and food rationing. Conditions on board were cramped, each man usually sleeping in a hammock slung below decks at his place of work, and toilet facilities were virtually non-existent.

JACK-OF-ALL-TRADES

A crew on an early exploration ship had to be completely self-sufficient, for they were often away at sea for several years and might go many months between landings. As well as being able to handle the ship sailors had to master other essential skills, such as carpentry, sailmaking, ropemaking, and cooking.

DISEASE

The most common form of disease encountered aboard ship was scurvy, a deficiency of vitamin C, caused by lack of fresh fruit and vegetables. The symptoms include bleeding into the skin and teeth loosening. Resistance to infection is also lowered, often resulting in death if untreated. All ships carried their share of rats, which might spread infectious diseases such as plague. Other common diseases were malaria, typhoid, and dysentery.

DRUNKENNESS

One of the commonest problems facing any captain commanding an early exploration ship on a long voyage was boredom and the unruly behavior of his crew. With fresh water in short supply the only drink available was beer (a gallon per crew member per day) or other stronger alcohols, which frequently led to drunkenness, not only on board but in port. Discipline was necessarily very harsh to avoid potentially fatal accidents at sea.

THE CHATHAM CHEST

After the Spanish Armada of 1588, so many seamen were wounded and maimed that Sir John Hawkins established the Chatham Chest— the first seamen's charity. All sailors in the Navy had to pay six pence a month from their wages into it for welfare purposes. This is the chest of 1625.

THE ART OF THE GUNNER

Most ships in the 16th to 18th centuries carried a number of cannon (an Elizabethan mortar is shown here), usually made from cast iron or bronze. They were mounted on carriages and secured in place by heavy ropes to control the recoil when being fired and to prevent them coming adrift in heavy seas. They were used mostly to disable a ship before boarding.

HEALTH & SAFETY

The health and safety of the crew aboard a typical ship in the early days of exploration was, to say the least, extremely hazardous. There were many accidents in simply carrying out the day-to-day tasks of sailing. Injuries sustained during encounters with enemy vessels, usually at close quarters, were horrific. Most ships carried a surgeon but the treatment he was able to administer was both limited and very crude. By far the most common form of treatment was the amputation of badly damaged or infected limbs. There was no anesthetic (other than to make the patient drunk) and the survival rate was appallingly low. Many of those who survived surgery died from gangrene afterward.

DAILY SUSTENANCE

All of the ship's food was prepared in the galley and then distributed among the crew. Food was rarely fresh and might consist of biscuit, salted beef or fish, supplemented by cheese and gruel, a kind of porridge mix. Drinking water was usually scarce but most ships carried a plentiful supply of beer. The pieces of tableware shown here were retrieved from Henry VIII's ship the *Mary Rose* and are typical of items in use throughout the Tudor period.

LIFE ON BOARD -A TIMELINE-

~1558~

The Spanish Armada sails against England with the intention of overthrowing Elizabeth I.

The Armada is defeated, but at great cost to the English forces.

~1590~

Sir John Hawkins and Sir Francis Drake found the Chatham Chest to support injured and disabled sailors.

~1594~

Sir John Hawkins founds the Hawkins Hospital, Chatham.

~1768~

The Admiralty commissions a refit of the Whitby collier, Endeavour, which is equipped to a relatively lavish extent with more and better provisions and improved sleeping conditions for the crew.

RIVALRY FOR EMPIRE

When Cook was born, the parts of the world conquered by European powers were still thought to belong to them. Empires provided precious metals like gold and silver, as well as timber and animal skins that could be used in trade. Spain thought that the Pacific Ocean was part of its empire, which spread from the Philippine islands in the west to central and southern America in the east. However, during wars against France and Spain, the British navy began to penetrate the Pacific, undermining the idea that it was a "Spanish lake." In 1740–1744, Commodore George Anson attacked Spanish shipping off the coast of California before returning home via China. British forces also started attacking Spanish bases, like Porto Bello, on the mainland of Central America.

COMMODORE GEORGE ANSON

In 1739, Britain and Spain began the War of Jenkins' Ear (so-called because a British merchant ship captain claimed a Spanish officer cut off his ear), and Anson took a squadron of five British naval vessels into the Pacific Ocean to attack Spanish shipping and settlements. He returned home around the world with plunder worth £400,000 ($700,000) but lost 1,051 of his 1,955 men, mainly from scurvy and other diseases.

A COMMEMORATIVE PLATE

Admiral Vernon's capture of the Spanish town of Porto Bello was celebrated in England, and many commemorative items were produced for sale. This plate, made in Lambeth or Liverpool in 1740, depicts the Iron Castle under bombardment, with the town beyond.

MODEL OF A CHINESE GARDEN

After crossing the Pacific Ocean, Anson put into the Canton River, China, in 1744, to refit his ship. His attitude was too aggressive for the Chinese, and his presence disturbed merchants trying to maintain trade. However, he was given this model Chinese garden, the contents of which signify long life and include a peach tree in coral, a pine tree in carved wood and ivory, bamboos in tinted ivory, and rocks in malachite and rose quartz.

THE TAKING OF THE NUESTRA *SEÑORA DE COVADONGA*

While in the Pacific, Anson captured one of the Spanish treasure ships sailing from Acapulco to Manila with 1,313,843 pieces of eight and 35,682 oz. of silver on board. Worth at least $700,000 then, it would be equivalent to many millions today.

SWORD SURRENDERED AT PORTO BELLO

This sword, with its Parisian hilt and Spanish blade, was surrendered by the Spanish commandant of the Iron Castle in 1739.

THE CAPTURE OF PORTO BELLO

In 1739, a British squadron under Admiral Vernon took the Spanish coastal town of Porto Bello in Central America. The town was defended by three castles, the first of which, the Iron Castle, was bombarded into submission.

Cook's Origins & Early Life

James Cook was born in a two-roomed cottage at Marton-in-Cleveland, north Yorkshire, England on October 7, 1728. His father was a Scottish laborer, his mother a Yorkshire woman, and they had seven children, of whom four died before they reached the age of five. James at first helped his father on a farm at Great Ayton, before being apprenticed to a grocer and haberdasher. Not liking shop work, he was apprenticed in 1746 to John Walker, a Whitby shipowner and captain in the coal trade, and spent the next nine years sailing from the River Tyne to London and the Baltic. Walker wanted to make him master of a ship, but instead, in 1755, Cook volunteered for the Royal Navy.

UNLOADING A COLLIER

Shipping coal was a hard, physical trade. Ships were loaded and unloaded by manpower. Coal had to be handled in baskets and is shown here being "whipped," or tipped down a chute. Cook managed these men and such work in the River Tyne and River Thames.

JAMES COOK, AGED 48

Cook became a naval captain and explorer of world fame. But his navigational ability was based on seafaring skills learned as a youth in the coal trade in the North Sea.

THE CUSTOMS HOUSE, LONDON

Cook would have known the London Customs House well. Although only cargo shipped from abroad was subject to import duty, coal from the northeast of England, carried down the east coast, still had to be declared.

THE PORT OF WHITBY

Whitby, where Cook went to sea, is on the northeast coast of England, where coal-mining close to the coast and River Tyne then made its shipment to London an important trade. Colliers were beached for loading and refitting.

A NORTH SEA COLLIER

This model of a "cat-built bark" shows the type of ship in the coal trade. A strong, roomy hull permitted it to rest on a beach or riverbed and carry a lot of cargo.

MASTER'S MATE

Britain was on the verge of war with France in June 1755 when Cook joined the 60-gun ship *Eagle* lying at Spithead, off Portsmouth. A month later, he was rated a Master's Mate. Two years later, he became a ship's master himself, sailing in the 64-gun *Pembroke* to assist the British to drive the French out of Canada. During the winter of 1758–1759 Cook helped perfect a chart of the Saint Lawrence River, which permitted an expedition under General James Wolfe to seize Quebec. At the mouth of the river, the waters around the island of Newfoundland were valuable for their cod, and after the war, each summer until 1767, Cook was employed making charts of the island.

A SEAMAN HEAVING THE LEAD

As the Master of a warship, Cook would often have relied on seamen sounding the depth of water beneath the ship's keel by casting a lead weight on a line over the side.

CHART OF NEWFOUNDLAND

This was one of the highly accurate charts made by James Cook and Michael Lane between 1763 and 1767. Cook did the surveying for these charts each summer, returning to London each winter to prepare the finished products for publication. Cook had married Elizabeth Betts in 1762 and lived in east London.

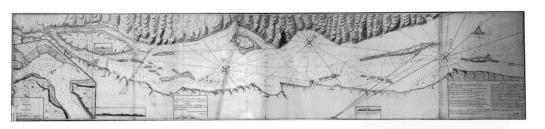

COOK'S CHART OF THE SAINT LAWRENCE RIVER

The chart that Cook prepared in 1758–1759 shows the numerous islands and shoals around which the army transports and naval escorts had to navigate in order to reach Quebec. Cook's chart opened the way for defeat of the French on the Heights of Abraham, which led to the British possession of Canada.

THE DEATH OF WOLFE IN QUEBEC

General Wolfe was shot in the battle for Quebec on September 13, 1759 and died after hearing of his victory. He was only 32 years old. His body is buried in Greenwich, London, where he lived, and where his statue now stands.

CAPTAIN COOK
-A TIMELINE-

~1756~

The Seven Years War starts between Britain and France

~1757~

Cook becomes a Master in the Royal Navy

~1758~

Cook perfects a chart of the Saint Lawrence River

~1759~

General Wolfe takes Quebec, Canada

~1762~

Cook marries Elizabeth Betts and lives in east London

~1763~

Cook begins charting the coastline of Newfoundland

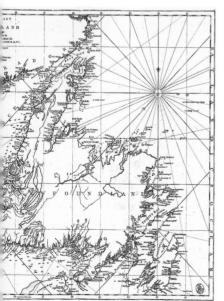

THEODOLITE 1737

When Cook charted Newfoundland, he worked in conjunction with surveyors led by Joseph Desbarres making maps on shore. Surveying instruments were already sophisticated. Theodolites, for measuring angles, had telescopic sights and rackwork circles for both the vertical and horizontal movements.

19

A PACIFIC VOYAGE

A PACIFIC VOYAGE

Cook was lucky in that his skills at navigation, surveying, and chart-making were noticed by Sir Hugh Palliser, another Yorkshireman, who was twice Cook's captain and subsequently Governor of Newfoundland, Comptroller of the Navy, and a member of the Board of Admiralty directed by Lord Sandwich. The latter presented Cook to George III, who was very interested in scientific discoveries. Indeed, in 1768, when the Royal Society wanted to measure the distance of Earth from the Sun by observing the "Transit of Venus" from somewhere in the southern Pacific, he helped finance the voyage. Cook was chosen to captain the ship sent to carry the scientists, who were led by Joseph Banks, later President of the Royal Society for forty years.

BANKS'S COLLECTIONS

As well as sailing with Cook to New Zealand and Australia, Banks traveled to Newfoundland and Iceland to develop this collection of natural history specimens. The collection became a foundation of that now in the Natural History Museum, in England.

JOSEPH BANKS

A wealthy young gentleman, Banks joined Cook's first voyage of exploration in the Pacific Ocean to pursue his natural history interests. He was President of the Royal Society from 1778 until 1820 and helped publish the journals of Cook's last voyage.

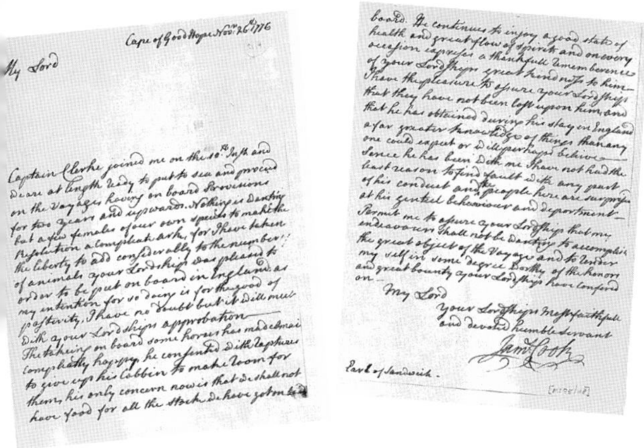

My Lord

Cape of Good Hope Novr 26th 1776

[handwritten letter, partly legible]

Earl of Sandwich.

LORD SANDWICH

Although better known for his indulgence in London life—his name was given to food he reputedly ordered to avoid leaving the gambling table—Sandwich was an accomplished administrator and First Lord of the Admiralty from 1770 until 1782. In this role, he promoted Cook after his second voyage and encouraged him to volunteer for the third. As Cook's letter to him in 1776 suggests, they became good friends, and after Cook's death, Sandwich presided over the publication of his journals.

ASTRONOMER AT HIS TRANSIT INSTRUMENT

The Astronomer Royal predicted the Transit of Venus across the face of the Sun in 1769 from repeated observations at the Royal Observatory, founded in 1675 in Greenwich Park, England. From there, nightly observations mapped the visible universe.

GEORGE III

George III became King in 1760, at the height of the Seven Years War with France. He had a political, as well as a scientific, interest in encouraging exploration, since France was intent on enlarging its empire. Significantly, though, Cook's last voyage was overshadowed by the rebellion of George III's American colonies, his journals for the voyage were published on the King's 48th birthday.

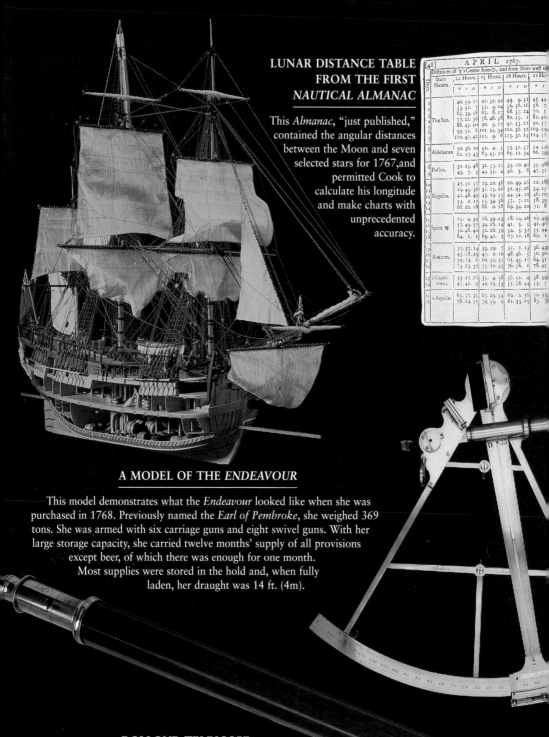

LUNAR DISTANCE TABLE FROM THE FIRST *NAUTICAL ALMANAC*

This *Almanac*, "just published," contained the angular distances between the Moon and seven selected stars for 1767, and permitted Cook to calculate his longitude and make charts with unprecedented accuracy.

A MODEL OF THE *ENDEAVOUR*

This model demonstrates what the *Endeavour* looked like when she was purchased in 1768. Previously named the *Earl of Pembroke*, she weighed 369 tons. She was armed with six carriage guns and eight swivel guns. With her large storage capacity, she carried twelve months' supply of all provisions except beer, of which there was enough for one month. Most supplies were stored in the hold and, when fully laden, her draught was 14 ft. (4m).

DOLLOND TELESCOPE

Cook applied to the Admiralty for a supply of navigational, chart-making, and astronomical instruments. Advances in the design of these instruments gave Cook the ability to navigate accurately and record his discoveries for posterity exactly. His navigational instruments included a telescope like this one made by Peter Dollond of London, who made the best available at the time. Since the 1750s telescopes had been made with an achromatic object glass that reduced the size of the telescope and rendered objects practically free of color distortion

PREPARATIONS

In April 1768 the Admiralty purchased the *Endeavour*, a three-year-old Whitby collier like those Cook had already sailed in the North Sea. She was only 106 ft. (32m) long on her upper deck, but her hull was strong enough to rest on shore to receive repairs, and capacious enough, with squeezing, to carry 94 people, victuals, stores, and equipment. While she was refitted in Deptford Dockyard, Cook obtained navigational equipment, now including the first Nautical Almanac, published by the Astronomer Royal in 1766. Meanwhile the Royal Society appointed naturalists to collect plants, artists to record what they saw, and an astronomer to observe the Transit of Venus.

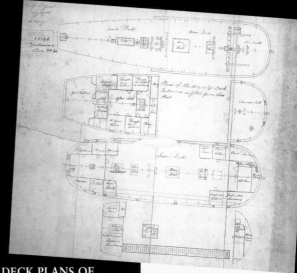

COOK'S SEXTANT

Oceanic navigation demanded an instrument that accurately measured the altitude of heavenly bodies. The backstaff, invented by John Davis in 1590, was still in use, but had been improved upon by John Hadley in 1734 with his quadrant or octant, and by the sextant in 1757. Cook took this sextant, made by Jesse Ramsden of London about 1770, on his third voyage.

DECK PLANS OF THE ENDEAVOUR

As generally in the navy, the ships' officers and senior civilians exercised on the quarterdeck. To accommodate the extra passengers, the decks of the *Endeavour* were subdivided into more cabins. The crew and civilian servants slept in hammocks slung above stores on the lower deck. The hold, containing further provisions, was reached through hatches covered by gratings.

CAPTAIN COOK - A TIMELINE -

~1766~

The first Nautical Almanac *published by the Astronomer Royal*

~1768~

A Whitby collier is purchased by the Navy for Cook's voyage and renamed Endeavour

Captain Wallis returns from the Pacific Ocean to England with information about Tahiti

The Endeavour *sails for Tahiti (July 30)*

LAUNCHING A SHIP AT DEPTFORD DOCKYARD

When the *Endeavour* was docked at Deptford, her hull was given an extra skin of wooden sheathing, her masts and yards were replaced, and partitions for extra cabins were inserted. After being refloated, she was rigged and equipped from the great storehouse. Food supplies were obtained from the Deptford victualling yard.

ENDEAVOUR

Cook's ship on his first voyage was sold in 1775 and broken up in 1793. For the last 30 years there have been attempts to build a replica, which was finally achieved at Fremantle in Australia between 1988 and 1994. She was built to the official plans in the National Maritime Museum and mainly by 18th-century methods, but using Australian timber and some modern techniques and artificial materials to enhance security of construction and rigging. Here she is shown over the Great Barrier Reef, which her predecessor struck in 1770, and on her voyage to Britain in 1997.

SAILING THE
ENDEAVOUR

Men set the sails as they did 200 years ago. The rigging employs over 700 pulleys called blocks. Here a seaman frees a snag on the main sail.

THE FURNITURE
AND EQUIPMENT

The Great Cabin (*right*) was shared by Cook with the naturalists and was where they did much of their botanical work. The officers' mess has a folding table copied from one owned by Cook. Everything looks as it did.

*Pictures courtesy of
HM Bark Endeavour Foundation, Fremantle*

CAPTAIN COOK
-A TIMELINE-

~1769~

The Transit of Venus is observed from Tahiti

Endeavour *searches for the Great Southern Continent*

Cook discovers and starts charting New Zealand

~1770~

Cook sails up the east coast of Australia

~1771~

Endeavour *returns to England (June 12). Cook is chosen to command a second voyage*

PORTABLE ASTRONOMICAL QUADRANT

To obtain an accurate measurement of the Transit of Venus, the observer's latitude and longitude had to be known precisely. Such accuracy could be achieved, along with other observations, by using the quadrant to measure the angular distance of the Sun, the Moon, or a star from the zenith—the point immediately overhead. This 12-inch portable quadrant, made by John Bird around 1768, is believed to have been taken by Cook on his first voyage.

PORTABLE OBSERVATORY

All the astronomical observations were made from a wood and canvas observatory, designed by Smeaton (who built the Eddystone Lighthouse) and constructed under the eye of Nevil Maskelyne, the Astronomer Royal.

COOK'S CHART OF NEW ZEALAND

Cook charted North and South Islands so exactly that their shapes, as he represented them, are almost identical to those derived from modern mapping techniques. Almost all the place names that he proposed are still in use today.

QUEEN CHARLOTTE SOUND, NEW ZEALAND

After charting North Island, New Zealand, Cook put into this deep coastal inlet, swathed in forest, with abundant supplies of fresh water, fish, wild celery, and scurvy grass. The local Maori, 300–400 in number, were poorer than those in the north. They introduced themselves with a

THE TRANSIT OF VENUS
& NEW ZEALAND
The First Voyage, 1768–1771

Cook and his companions set sail to observe the Transit of Venus in July 1768. They made for Tahiti, an island in the Pacific Ocean discovered by Captain Wallis, who had just returned from circumnavigating the globe before they set sail. The observations were successfully accomplished in June 1769, when Cook followed secret orders to look for the Great Southern Continent. Exploring south and west, the *Endeavour* discovered New Zealand, which Cook sailed all around. Repairs were effected in Queen Charlotte Sound, where the Maori were friendly and helpful. The charts Cook was to produce were not to be improved for another century.

ASTRONOMICAL CLOCK

In 1769, observers of the Transit of Venus in different parts of the world had to note the time that the planet appeared to touch the disk of the Sun. Absolute accuracy of timing was essential. Thus, when observations were made, a regulating clock was set up inside the portable observatory on shore. The clock was also used to check the running of marine chronometers. Its own accuracy had been checked by the Astronomer Royal at Greenwich before the voyage. The clock shown here went on at least one of Cook's voyages and is inscribed "Royal Society No. 35 John Shelton, London."

GREGORIAN
REFLECTING TELESCOPE

To ensure accurate and comparable observations of the Transit of Venus, the Royal Society issued similar telescopes to all the observers that it dispatched to different parts of the world. This reflecting telescope was made in 1763 in London by James Short. Cook was equipped with two of them.

AUSTRALIA
The First Voyage, 1768–1771

Cook sailed west from New Zealand to explore Australia. Dutchmen had discovered the west coast, which they named New Holland, and the island of Tasmania more than 150 years before. However, the east coast was still unknown. Sighting its southern end, Cook sailed north, stopping to water in a bay so full of specimens for the naturalists that they called it Botany Bay. Farther north, the *Endeavour* suddenly struck on part of the Great Barrier Reef. Disembarking with difficulty, the ship had to be beached for six weeks for repairs. Before sailing home, Cook claimed the entire coast of New South Wales for King George III.

AUSTRALIAN FISH

Fish caught by the seamen and naturalists were both eaten and studied. The former enthusiastically helped the latter. The *Arripis Trutta*, shown here, grows to 3 ft. (1m) long and was caught in the waters of Australia and New Zealand.

A KANGAROO

While repairing in the Endeavour River, they saw animals "around the size of a grayhound, slender, mouse-colored, swift, with a long tail, jumping like a hare." They outpaced Banks's grayhound, but several were shot and eaten. This one was painted by Sydney Parkinson.

THE ENDEAVOUR UNDER REPAIR

After the *Endeavour* got off the Great Barrier Reef, Cook found the 'Endeavour River' where the ship could be unloaded and beached for the repair of her hull.

AUSTRALIAN FLOWER

While the *Endeavour* was under repair, Joseph Banks gathered more specimens of plants and flowers, which were later presented to the British Museum. This one was called *Solanum viride*.

BOTANY BAY

Cook's first landing on Australian soil was in Botany Bay, where much of the vegetation and bird and animal life, was quite new. They met Aborigines and caught large stingrays. Cook named the bay after the great quantity of botanical specimens collected by Joseph Banks and the botanist Daniel Solander.

QUARTERDECK OF A NAVAL VESSEL IN THE TROPICS

To shelter a ship's officers from the sun, canvas awnings were rigged over the quarterdeck. Common seamen were excluded from this deck unless performing some duty. Animals, taken to supply food, often became pets. This picture was painted around 1775 on a voyage from the West Indies to England, but the quarterdeck of the *Endeavour* probably looked similar as she made her way up the east coast of Australia. Note the goat (for milk). Cook also took a goat—which had already sailed once around the world with Wallis!

THE GREAT SOUTHERN CONTINENT
The Second Voyage, 1772–1775

Cook's first voyage had not disproved the existence of a Great Southern Continent, and another expedition was soon equipped to solve this question. On July 13, 1772, this time with two ships, the *Resolution* and *Adventure*, Cook sailed for the Cape of Good Hope and then voyaged east through fog and ice, sleet and snow, at around latitude 60°. Turning north, the two ships met at a rendezvous in Dusky Sound, New Zealand. Cook was able to find destinations precisely because he had been given the first accurate marine chronometer with which to find his longitude. The following Antarctic summer, 1773–1774, Cook again sailed back into the ice and snow, reaching 71° and finally proving that a habitable southern continent really did not exist.

PICKERSGILL HARBOUR, DUSKY SOUND, NEW ZEALAND

Returning from Antarctic waters in March 1773, Cook moored the *Resolution* in a small creek "so near the shore as to reach it by a large tree which growed in a horizontal direction over the water so long that the top of it reached our gunwale." The creek had plentiful supplies of fresh water and fish, to the delight of the seamen. One can be seen here returning from the astronomical observation tent that was set up on shore.

PICKING UP ICE

Voyaging through Antarctic waters, Cook's crews replenished their water supply by cutting ice from icebergs, which they called "ice islands." In the absence of land in these latitudes, they also shot sea birds to obtain fresh meat. Hodges drew the scene in January 1773.

COOK'S CHRONOMETER

At his fourth attempt, John Harrison succeeded in making a practical and reliable marine chronometer. It was tested on a sea voyage in 1761 and over four weeks was out by only five seconds. However, Harrison was awarded only half the Board of Longitude's £20,000 ($35,000) prize; for the chronometer also had to be capable of precise reproduction. In 1772, Cook therefore took with him this copy by Larcum Kendall, on trial. Its accuracy permitted Harrison to get the other half of his prize in 1773.

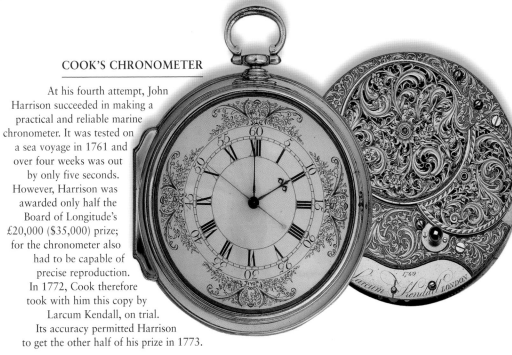

THE CAPE OF GOOD HOPE

Cook was accompanied on this voyage by the 28-year old artist William Hodges, who painted this view from the deck of the *Resolution* on their voyage south. The *Adventure* can be seen inshore, with her sails aback and Cape Town behind. Hodges was to paint many more dramatic landscapes during the voyage.

MAORI CLUB AX

Although generally friendly, the Maori peoples of New Zealand could be dangerous. In December 1773, Captain Furneaux in the *Adventure* missed a rendezvous with Cook's *Resolution*, leaving his ship alone in Queen Charlotte Sound, New Zealand. The ship's cutter and ten men were sent to get provisions, but they were all killed and some were eaten. In their attack, the Maori probably used a club ax of the type shown.

31

THE PACIFIC PEOPLES . . .
The Second Voyage, 1772–1775

TAHITIAN FLAPS

This long-haired fly swat—"very ingeniously wrought"— was obtained by trade by Joseph Banks from an island close to Tahiti; the flanking figures are handles.

During the Antarctic winters, Cook explored and charted many of the islands of the Pacific Ocean. Both in 1773 and 1774, he was welcomed back to Tahiti, where a favorite anchorage was Matavai Bay. In 1773, the crews of both *Resolution* and *Adventure* were sick with scurvy, and Cook spread a sail as an awning on the beach, where the sick could recover in comfort. The hills inland gave the artist of the voyage, William Hodges, perfect subject matter. The splendor of the scenes that he painted did a lot to make Europeans think that the Pacific islands were paradise. The Tahitians were depicted in noble, classical poses, but Cook suffered a lot from their eagerness to acquire items from the ships, by theft if not trade.

Resolution *and* Adventure *in Matavai Bay, Tahiti, in 1773; by William Hodges.*

OMAI

Omai was from Huahine, near Tahiti. Intelligent and friendly, he acted as an interpreter and wished to visit Britain. Captain Furneaux in the Adventure brought him back to London, where he became a celebrity before being returned to Tahiti in 1777.

BAKING BREADFRUIT

The breadfruit tree grows naturally in Tahiti. The Tahitians eat the fruit and are shown here cooking it. Joseph Banks proposed growing the fruit in the West Indies to feed plantation slaves. William Bligh, who accompanied Cook on his second voyage, delivered the trees in 1791, but the slaves shunned the fruit because of its bland taste.

TAHITIAN WAR GALLEYS

At Tahiti in 1774, Cook came across the assembled fleet of war canoes and galleys—more than 300 vessels—drawn up for inspection by the principal chief. They carried flags and streamers and "made a grand and noble appearance such as was never seen before in this sea." Cook watched as, lashed together in divisions, they practiced paddling furiously to land together on the beach, where they engaged in mock battle. After William Hodges had drawn them, Cook had the pleasure of going on board several of the fleet.

CAPTAIN COOK
-A TIMELINE-

~1772–1773~

Resolution *and* Adventure *search for the Great Southern Continent*

~1773~

Resolution *circles the South Pacific, discovering the Tonga island*

~1773–74~

Cook reaches latitude 71°, looking for the Great Southern Continent

~1774~

A wider Pacific circle discovers Easter Island, the Marquesas, and the New Hebrides

~1775~

Cook returns to England (July 30)

FOUR TONGAN WAR CLUBS

Although the Tongan people were friendly to Cook, their chieftains had to defend their islands. Because they traveled and fought from canoes, paddles sometimes served as war clubs. These clubs are thought to have been collected by Cook, probably by trade, for the Tongan people had an insatiable appetite for nails. Cook's voyages were the first to bring back collections of such ethnographic items, giving rise to comparisons and the study of anthropology.

THE LANDING IN EROMANGA, NEW HEBRIDES

In August 1774, Cook landed to ask for wood and water but was met by a great group armed with clubs, darts, stones, bows, and arrows. He suspected the worst and stepped back into his boat, upon which the crowd surged forward, shooting and throwing missiles and tried to drag the boat up the beach. Cook's musket misfired and he had to order others to fire. Four men fell, but Cook's boat escaped.

. . . THE PACIFIC PEOPLES
The Second Voyage, 1772–1775

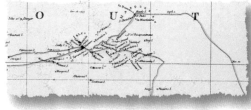

Exploring west of Tahiti in 1773, Cook discovered the Tonga island group, where the people were so friendly that he called them the Friendly Islands. Farther east in 1774, he found Easter Island, with its giant statues, and the Marquesas, islands known to the Spaniards but whose location had never been charted. Returning west again, he found the New Hebrides, inhabited by Melanesians and less friendly than the Polynesians so far encountered. These island groups had a special beauty, with many unusual flowering trees and shrubs, including the breadfruit tree. However, drinking water was often scarce, while underwater coral reefs made navigation perilous. Cook's achievement was even greater, and he was to be highly honored on his return home.

THE MONUMENTS OF EASTER ISLAND

In March 1774, Cook sent 27 men to explore the island. They found seven stone figures, four of which were still standing, with three overturned, perhaps by earthquakes. The figures represented men to their waist, with large ears. They were around 18 ft. (5.5m) high and 5 ft. (1.5m) wide, "ill-shaped," and had large "hats" of red rock on their heads, like some Egyptian gods. One hat measured over 5 ft. (1.5m) in diameter. The figures appeared to mark burial places, for among the stones were several human bones, as shown in Hodges' painting.

THE PACIFIC FURTHER EXPLORED
The Third Voyage, 1776–1780

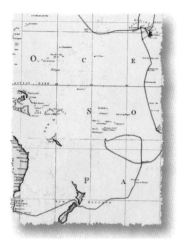

In July 1776, one year after returning home, Cook sailed again for the Pacific Ocean. This was partially to return Omai to Tahiti, partially because there was hope of finding a North-West Passage from the Pacific to the Atlantic for trading purposes, and partially to examine some desolate islands discovered by the French, Britain's enemy, near the Cape of Good Hope. The *Resolution* and *Discovery*, his two ships, made for Tasmania (then known as Van Diemen's Land) and New Zealand, before sailing through the Tonga islands to Tahiti. Aiming for the west coast of Canada, Cook pressed north at the end of the year, spending Christmas 1777 on a coral atoll, Christmas Island, before discovering the Sandwich Islands, including Hawaii.

STONE TOOLS AND TATTOOING INSTRUMENTS, TAHITI

The tools and instruments in use in the Pacific islands were Stone-Age in their sophistication. European society, which took the Bible literally, assumed that primitive societies were closer to nature and to the innocence of the Garden of Eden. However, the islanders' practice of human sacrifice, their freer morals and thefts from Cook's ships, conflicted with Christian ideals and made Europeans question their own literal beliefs.

KENDALL'S THIRD MARINE CHRONOMETER

Cook continued to benefit from the rapid improvement of navigational equipment. In the *Discovery*, he took another chronometer made by Larcum Kendall, who had been requested by the Board of Longitude to attempt to improve upon his previous copies of John Harrison's prize-winning model. The new "watch machine" was simpler, and mass production would permit merchant shipping and traders to follow where Cook had been.

A HUMAN SACRIFICE IN TAHITI

On his fourth visit to Tahiti, Cook was honored by being taken to a human sacrifice intended to assist the chief in a local war. He made careful observations. No women were present, and Cook had to remove his hat. Drums were beaten, and prayers were uttered. A man, bruised from being beaten to death, was trussed to a pole. One of his eyes was ceremoniously eaten, before he was buried; then a dog was sacrificed and presented to their atua, or god.

A NIGHT DANCE BY WOMEN IN TONGA,
OR THE FRIENDLY ISLES

Making his third visit to the Friendly Isles, Cook was entertained as an honored guest. The Tongan men sat in a semicircle and began a song with a rhythm beaten with hollow pieces of bamboo. Then younger women came and encircled the men, singing and dancing, their bodies shining in the torchlight: "the most beautiful forms that imagination can conceive." Quickening songs interspersed with savage shouts made it an exhilarating performance.

CAPTAIN COOK
-A TIMELINE-

~1776~

Cook begins his third Pacific voyage and sails south in the Resolution, *in company with the* Discovery *(July 12)*

Britain's American colonies declare their independence

~1777~

Cook returns to New Zealand, Tonga, and Tahiti and discovers Christmas Island

~1778~

After discovering Hawaii, Cook explores the northwest coast of North America and passes through the Bering Strait

37

THE NOOTKA SOUND PEOPLE

Large numbers of native people visited the ships daily, some clearly having come from a long distance. On first appearance, they generally went through the same ceremony. They first paddled with all their strength around the ships; a chief, his face covered with a mask of either a human or an animal face, then stood up with a spear or rattle in his hand and shouted a greeting. Sometimes this was followed by a song in which they all joined and made "very agreeable harmony," upon which they came closer and began to trade.

POLAR BEAR

Cook's companions spotted a white bear in the arctic. John Webber, the artist, was only 24 when they set out, but he was accomplished at rapidly drawing broad landscapes and natural objects with precise detail. Here, he caught the huge size and dangerous character of the animal.

REFITTING THE SHIPS

The *Resolution*'s fore and mizzen masts had to be replaced, and the rigging of her mainmast had to be renewed. Sheer legs were thus set up on the *Resolution*'s deck to get out the defective masts. New masts were cut and made on shore, where smiths forged new fittings on the beach.

A SEA OTTER

The sea otter's lustrous skins were highly prized. Russian traders had been busy buying the pelts from Innuit and Native Americans since 1741, when Bering discovered the strait that bears his name. The Chinese paid high prices for them. Cook's report of the trade prompted British merchants in China, then other Europeans and Americans, to mount trading ventures. Soon the north Pacific was alive with ships.

NORTHWEST CANADA & ALASKA
The Third Voyage, 1776–1780

Off the Canadian coast early in 1778, Cook first found a safe bay, later called Nootka Sound, (below left) in which to refit the *Resolution* and *Discovery*. He then coasted north, entering every inlet in search of a Northwest Passage. Everywhere he landed, Cook met the Native American people who lived on these coasts. Rounding Alaska, he pressed through the Bering Strait dividing the continents of Asia and America and, peering through persistent fog, entered the Arctic Sea. At 20°, he met the pack ice and, unwilling to let his ships get trapped, turned back. Planning to return the next summer, he then sailed for the Sandwich Islands, where Hawaii seemed to offer a welcoming winter resting place.

SURVEY WORK

As soon as the ships were moored, the portable observatories were set up on an elevated rock for the astronomers to make their observations. The longitude of the cove was settled with the highest care, for this position would become a bearing for further navigation. In front of the tents, surveying work began, to chart and map the waters and terrain of the sound.

BEAVER BOWL, INLAID WITH SHELL

The indians brought fish, furs, weapons, bladders full of oil, and even human skulls to exchange for any type of metal— knives, chisels, nails, and buttons. They stole as well as traded, and even Cook's own gold watch was taken, though later recovered. The greatest desire of the seamen was for sea-otter pelts. This wooden bowl, carved in the shape of a beaver, was probably obtained in Nootka Sound.

SHOOTING "SEA-HORSES"

Penetrating through the Bering Strait in August 1778, in latitude 20°, Cook met an ice field, inhabited by "sea-horses," or walrus. To obtain fresh meat, boats were sent from both ships to kill 12 of the great beasts. Cook was delighted and, to ensure that the meat was eaten, stopped all normal rations except bread.

THE DEATH OF COOK

In Hawaii, Cook was greeted like a god. The Hawaiians were expecting their god, Lono, to arrive on a floating island with trees, not unlike the *Resolution*. Gifts and trade abounded, but so also did thefts. Cook tried to punish the culprits and retrieve stolen equipment, sometimes by taking hostages. By February 1779, awe for Cook, and his own patience, had both grown thin. While trying to retrieve a stolen ship's cutter, Cook was suddenly killed. Captain Clerke of the *Discovery* finished looking for the Northwest Passage but was unsuccessful. Cook's voyages had nevertheless opened up the largest ocean in the world to European trade and settlement. They had contributed to knowledge of different peoples and cultures, of Earth, its plants and animals, and of its place in the universe. In addition, they had been achieved with little loss of seamen's lives and respect for other races. Cook set new standards for all explorers to follow.

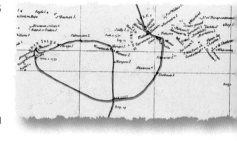

HAWAIIAN SPEAR

The Hawaiians, like other Pacific islanders, originally had only wood and stone weapons, against which they defended themselves with woven mats. These were no match for European firearms and swords made of metal. However, realizing the usefulness of metal, they traded and stole it whenever possible and made metal daggers. Cook was stabbed with one in the struggle before his death. Otherwise, the crowd by which he was overwhelmed was armed with spears and stones.

THE DEATH OF COOK

When the *Discovery*'s cutter was taken on February 14, 1779, Cook went ashore to take the local chief hostage for its return. A hostile crowd gathered, which grew angrier when Cook himself fired at a man who threatened him, upon which the Hawaiians launched themselves on Cook's party. Cook was hit from behind with a club, then stabbed and drowned.

COOK'S SUCCESSOR IN THE PACIFIC OCEAN

In 1789, William Bligh, sailing master of the *Resolution* on the second voyage, suffered a mutiny after returning to Tahiti in the Bounty to collect breadfruit for the West Indies.

COOK UNDERMINED

Cook normally treated the Pacific islanders with reasoned patience. In Hawaii, however, he started to act out of character and decided on a sudden descent on the Hawaiian village. He took armed marines and ordered their firearms to be loaded and fired to kill. It is now thought that strain and the poor diet of three long voyages, and possibly illness, had undermined his understanding and caution.

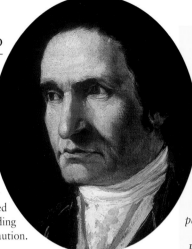

BRITISH PISTOL

This pistol was the sort issued to sea officers, and Cook would have carried one as necessity. When he was killed, he was carrying a two-barreled musket, one barrel loaded with "small shot," the other with ball. He was accompanied by a lieutenant and nine marines, all armed with muskets. The number of guns was intended to threaten. The disadvantage of these weapons in a crowd situation was that they could not be reloaded quickly.

POEDUA—A HOSTAGE

In November 1777, two seamen deserted in the Society Islands, and to force the islanders to return them, Cook took hostage the 15-year-old daughter of the local chief, her brother, and her husband. Among friends, the three captives were not alarmed, but their father quickly secured the deserters. John Webber painted the girl's portrait.

DID YOU KNOW?

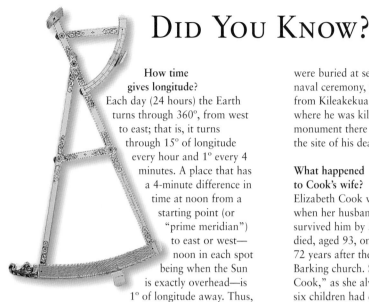

How time gives longitude?

Each day (24 hours) the Earth turns through 360°, from west to east; that is, it turns through 15° of longitude every hour and 1° every 4 minutes. A place that has a 4-minute difference in time at noon from a starting point (or "prime meridian") to east or west—noon in each spot being when the Sun is exactly overhead—is 1° of longitude away. Thus, accurate east/west time variations between places can be converted into relative distances and positions of longitude.

Where the design of ships like the *Endeavour* came from?

The "cat-built" ships constructed for the coal trade on the north-east coast of England in Cook's day, were based on types captured from the Dutch in the Anglo-Dutch wars of 1652–74. Because of their shallow waters and the need to load and unload vessels sitting on the foreshore, and because the Dutch grew rich from carrying bulky cargoes round the world, they designed very strong, flat-bottomed, roomy ships which proved ideal as a pattern for later English colliers.

Where Cook is buried?

The Hawaiians partly ate then burnt Cook's body, according to custom. A few days later, when relations with his men had improved, they returned most of his bones. On February 21, 1779, his remains were buried at sea in a full naval ceremony, just offshore from Kileakekua Bay where he was killed. A monument there marks the site of his death.

What happened to Cook's wife?

Elizabeth Cook was 38 when her husband died. She survived him by 56 years and died, aged 93, on May 13, 1835, 72 years after their marriage in Barking church. She remained deeply proud of "Mr Cook," as she always spoke of him. Sadly, all their six children had died by 1794.

What ships the Europeans used as trading vessels?

In the first part of the 16th century the carrack became the most popular European ship for trade, exploration, and warfare. Carracks became important symbols of national pride. In England, Henry VIII had built the *Great Harry*, which was the largest carrack built up until that time. The French responded by building *La Grande Françoise* which was even larger. Sadly, it was so large that it could not get out of the mouth of the harbor where it was built. By the end of the 16th century the carrack was being replaced by the galleon. By Cook's time, a wider variety of vessels was used, including the "cat-built" craft such as the *Endeavour*.

Who made up a ship's crew?

Most ships not only had ordinary sailors amongst the crew but also carpenters, priests, cooks, doctors, gunners, blacksmiths, pilots, and boys as young as ten years of age on board. Crew members normally came from many different countries and the captain sometimes had difficulty making them understand his instructions, because they spoke so many different languages.

What the biggest problem faced by sailors was?

The main problem faced by sailors on long voyages was scurvy. This often fatal disease is caused by a lack of vitamin C which comes from fresh fruit and vegetables. Fresh food did not last long on the ships of the explorers. Sailors would become extremely tired and would start to bleed from the scalp and the gums. However it was not until 1915 that vitamins were identified. Citrus fruit juice (ascorbic acid) was adopted against scurvy by the Admiralty in 1795 but before that fresh air, dry clothing, warmth, and exercise were also thought to help prevent it. There was thus much confusion about its exact cause.

Where the term "a square meal" comes from?

It is not known when this term first came into use but since at least Tudor times meals on board ship were dished up on square platters, which seamen balanced on their laps. They had frames around the edge to prevent the food from falling off and were so shaped to enable them to be easily stored when not in use. Each sailor thus received his full ration, or square meal, for the day.

Do we still use the stars for navigation?

It is easy to assume that because navigational techniques used in the past were relatively simple they were also inaccurate. This is not necessarily true, although results need to be accurately recorded and verified to be usable. In 1967 astronomers discovered pulsars, rapidly rotating condensed stars (formed from dead stars) that emit radio waves, or pulses, as detectable beams. They pulsate at fixed rates making it possible for future space programs to utilize them for navigational purposes in outer space.

GLOSSARY

amber Fossil tree resin, *(see below)* which is usually orange-brown in color. Amber is often used in jewelry.

amputation The surgical removal of a limb or body part.

anesthetic A drug that causes temporary loss of sensation in the body.

armada A large fleet of warships.

arrears An unpaid debt that is overdue.

astronomical Relating to the study of the Universe beyond the Earth.

awning A canopy-like covering attached to the exterior of a building to provide shelter.

baptism A Christian ceremony that signifies spiritual cleansing and rebirth.

bombardment The heavy, continuous attacking of a target with artillery.

botany The scientific study of plants and vegetation.

cannibal A person who eats the flesh of other humans.

"cat boat" A large vessel often used in the coal trade. The origins of the name are a mystery, but one theory is that the name comes from coal and timber—which these boats often transported.

charter To lease or rent services and possessions; a document issued by an authority that grants an institution certain rights or privileges.

charting Navigational mapping of coastlines and seas so that sailors can find routes for purposes of trade and exploration.

circumnavigate To travel all the way around something by ship.

civil war A war between different groups in the same country.

colonization The extension of a nation's power by the establishment of settlements and by trade in foreign lands.

commission A committee set up to deal with and look at a certain issue.

dead-reckoning A way of estimating one's current position based on a known previous position, allowing for speed, distance, and direction moved.

deck A platform built on a ship. There are often numerous decks within a ship.

dissolution The process of breaking up and destroying something. The "Dissolution of the Monasteries" was a process undertaken by King Henry VIII between 1536 and 1540, which resulted in the disbanding of all monasteries, nunneries, and friaries, and the claiming of their income, wealth, and land for the king.

draught The depth to which a ship sinks in the water, measured from its keel.

dysentery An inflammatory infection of the intestines resulting in severe diarrhea. Dysentery was a major cause of death on board ship.

electrical charge Electrical energy that has been stored.

equator The imaginary line running around the center of the Earth from east to west, at an equal distance from the North and South Poles.

expulsion The act of forcing something or someone out.

Global Positioning System Satellite system that allows users to pinpoint their location.

haberdasher A person who sells small items for sewing, such as needles, buttons, and thread.

hawkbells Bells attached to the legs of a hawk by a small leather strap, just above the talons. Bells were often organized to ring with different tones, so that in a group of hawks a pleasant sound would be produced. Hawking was a popular country sport where the hawk hunted for its owner.

hulk A ship that is afloat, but is not capable of

going to sea. It often refers to a ship that has had its rigging or equipment removed.

interior The inland part of a country.

junk A Chinese sailing ship.

keel The structural main beam running down the middle of a ship, serving as the spine of the boat's structure.

kingdom A country with a king or queen at its head.

latitude The imaginary parallel lines running east to west around the Earth.

longitude The imaginary parallel lines running north to south around the Earth.

malaria A disease spread by the bite of a mosquito.

missionary A person who tries to convert native inhabitants to their own religious viewpoint. Missionaries often provide charitable services.

mortality The likelihood of death. The mortality rate is the rate of death in a certain number of people in a population.

musket A muzzle-loading smoothbore gun (without rotational grooves to guide the projectile along the barrel) mounted in and fired from the shoulder.

mutiny A rebellion by members of a ship's crew to overthrow the captain.

native A person born in a particular place or country, and living there.

observatory A building designed and equipped for looking at the stars and for watching astronomical events.

pack-ice A large collection of ice that has combined to form a single mass. Pack-ice moves with the currents of the sea.

patronage The support, encouragement, and backing (often financial) of a person or people.

piracy Stealing whilst at sea; taking ships and possessions without the instruction of a sovereign or ruler.

primitive Relating to an early stage of technical or technological progress; a person who belongs to an early stage of civilized advancement.

purser The person on board a ship who is responsible for all things financial.

putrefaction The decomposition or breakdown of a dead creature.

pyramid A building or structure with triangular sides narrowing to a peak at the top.

sheer-legs A temporary structure of two or three tied beams, that formed a support for lifting heavy weights.

Spanish Inquisition The Spanish Inquisition was set up in 1478 by Ferdinand and Isabella of Spain. Its purpose was to ensure that Catholic orthodoxy was maintained in Spain.

Spanish Main The mainland coast of the Spanish Empire around the Caribbean area.

strait A narrow sea-channel, joining two larger bodies of water.

subdue To put down or contain by force or by authority.

sugar cane A tall fibrous grass-like plant, that naturally contains high levels of sucrose, which is refined to produce sugar.

tribute The tax system employed by the Aztecs to support their state. This was paid by all the regions under their control to finance building, military, nobility, and religion.

typhoid An illness caused by eating or drinking contaminated food or water.

zealous Filled with enthusiasm and energy in favor of a cause.

zenith The point directly above a certain location.

FURTHER READING
& WEBSITES

BOOKS

Atlas of Exploration
Andrew Kerr and Francois Naude (Dorling Kindersley Publications, 2008)

Captain Cook: Great Explorer of the Pacific (Great Explorers of the World)
Stephen Feinstein (Enslow Publishers, 2010)

Captain James Cook
Richard Hough (Coronet Books, 2003)

Captain James Cook (Great Explorers)
William W. Lace (Chelsea House Publications, 2009)

Captain James Cook Three Times Around the World (Great Explorations)
Milton Meltzer (Benchmark Books (NY), 2001)

Explorer (Eyewitness)
Rupert Matthews (Dorling Kindersley Publications, 2003)

Explorers & Exploration
Steadwell Books and Lara Rice Bergen (Heinemann Library, 2001)

Explorers of the South Pacific: A Thousand Years of Exploration, from the Polynesians to Captain Cook and Beyond
Daniel E. Harmon (Mason Crest Publishers, 2002)

James Cook (Explorers Set 1)
Kristin Petrie (Checkerboard Books, 2004)

James Cook: The Pacific Coast and Beyond
R. A. Beales (Crabtree Publishing Company, 2005)

New York Public Library Amazing Explorers: A Book of Answers for Kids
Brendan January (Wiley, 2001)

Polar Explorers for Kids: Historic Expeditions to the Arctic and Antarctic with 21 Activities
Maxine Snowden (Chicago Review Press, 2003)

Tools of Navigation: A Kid's Guide to the History and Science of Finding Your Way (Tools of Discovery)
Rachel Dickinson (Nomad Press, 2005)

You Wouldn't Want to Travel with Captain Cook!: A Voyage You'd Rather Not Make
Mark Bergin (Children's Press (CT), 2006)

You Are the Explorer
Nathan Aaseng (Oliver Press, 1999)
Vancouver: University of British Columbia Press, 2005
0774811897

WEBSITES

www.captcook-ne.co.uk/ccne/who.htm
An excellent and detailed biographical site with timeline, family tree, and video presentation of the life of Captain James Cook.

www.south-pole.com/p0000071.htm
An account of Cook's second voyage to the Antarctic to establish whether this unexplored part of the southern hemisphere contained another continent.

www.nmm.ac.uk/captain-cook
The National Maritime Museum, London, site with a biography and details about Cook's voyages and the ships, seafarers, and life at sea of the time.

www.bbc.co.uk/history/british/empire_seapower/captaincook_01.shtml
This BBC site has detailed descriptions of all of Cook's voyages as well as of his scientific discoveries and their benefits to the world.

www.nma.gov.au/cook/index.php
A site that shows and describes a collection of more than 300 artefacts brought back by Cook from his voyages that give an insight into Pacific island culture.

http://southseas.nla.gov.au/journals/banks/contents.html
The Endeavour journal of the naturalist Joseph Banks, August 25, 1768 to July 12, 1771.

http://academickids.com/encyclopedia/index.php/James_Cook
An encyclopedic biography of Captain Cook with great cross-referencing to subjects related to his voyages.

www.kidskonnect.com/subject-index/16-history/265-explorers.html
A gateway to sites about the different explorers.

INDEX

ACKNOWLEDGMENTS

Consultant Editor: Pieter van der Merwe, National Maritime Museum.
We would like to thank: Graham Rich, Tracey Pennington, and
Deon Fullard for their assistance.

For further information on the subjects/pictures in this book contact:
National Maritime Museum, Greenwich, London SE10 9NF, UK.
www.nmm.ac.uk

NOTE TO READERS
The website addresses are correct at the time of publishing. However, due to
the ever-changing nature of the Internet, websites and content may change.
Some websites can contain links that are unsuitable for children. The publisher
is not responsible for changes in content or website addresses. We advise
that Internet searches should be supervised by an adult.